# THE
# BALANCING
# ACT

## KEEPING "FIRST-THINGS" FIRST

## A Guide To Work & Life Balance

### Written By
### J. Harrison Blackwell

# The Balancing Act
## Keeping "First Things" First

Original copyright © 2004, revised 2006 by J. Harrison
Blackwell

Printed in the United States of America.

Cataloging-in-Publication data is on file with The Library of
Congress.    2006938852

ISBN:  0-9771640-2-0

Publisher:    Visions + Solutions
              P.O. Box 5162
              Midlothian, VA   23112
              Phone:  804-639-9886
              Fax:     804-639-9884
              E-mail:  jbvisions@aol.com
              Web Site:  www.jhbvisions.com

Editor -  Allen Lewis - Richmond, VA
Book Cover Design by Mike Schrum - Tri-Cedar
        Digital Imaging – Midlothian, VA

# THE
# BALANCING
# ACT

## KEEPING "FIRST-THINGS" FIRST

# Acknowledgements

Special thanks - to my friends and family members with whom I have spent many hours talking about this subject. Our discussions on - raising our children, finding time for ourselves and significant others has inspired me to share my solutions with others.

Most importantly, to my children, Robert Michael and Christina, thank you for hanging in there with me when I wasn't balancing things very well. Your patience and loving support helped me make it through – I love you with all my heart and soul. Many thanks to your father for being there for you when I wasn't - it was a team effort.

To my Literary Coach, Renee Bobb - you have been a Godsend, your patience and persistence kept me on track. I'd still be updating and making changes to the book if it were not for you.

Lastly, to my reviewers, Simone Nicholas, Sonya Johnson, Shelle Ashley-Cleveland, Susan Chapman, Ronald Carrington, Dena Hembrick-Chouquette and Cherrie Davis. Thank you for your honest, candid feedback and suggestions.

*God Bless You All*

# Table of Contents

# Preface

This book is dedicated to anyone struggling to balance work, family and personal obligations. You can be male, female, single, married, with or without children. It doesn't matter. If you feel you never have enough time to do what you want to do and its causing you to feel frustrated, tired, stressed and ready to pull out your hair – Hold on. I have something that may help you.

In case you're wondering if I am an expert on balancing work and family, I am not. Who am I? I am one, like many, who struggled to find the answer to the question - How do I get everything done at work and home without losing my mind or the attention and love of my family and still have time for myself? I can't count the number of times I either rehearsed to myself or simply exclaimed, "I just can't balance work and family." I said it so much that it's exactly what I got – an inability to balance the two. I was close to exhaustion before I realized how I was confessing on a daily basis what I could not do. However, somewhere deep inside I believed it was possible. I just couldn't give up trying.

This book is a composite of the number of things I tried throughout my career to gain control of this part of my life. I read many books and sought advice from many in the same position as myself. I can remember only one person who worked with me who had seemed to master this feat. As I observed her I noticed one consistent thing. She stuck to her goals and always kept her family first. From the peaceful look that was always upon her face - I knew she had balance. In my determination to obtain the same, I had to make some tough decisions. So will you. Do I regret any of them? Absolutely not!

I

The art of balancing work and family must be personalized. It's not a one-size fit all approach. What may work for one isn't guaranteed to work for another. YOU have to find what's best for you. However, I hope my experiences, stories, trials and failures will help you find your way to obtaining balance in your life. When you do, and you will, be sure to share with others how you find balance.

Reading this book is actually a step in the right direction to invoke a positive change in your lifestyle. However, don't stop with just reading it!

I have included several exercises to help you think through and experiment with the solutions that worked for me. **Take the time to complete these exercises** since truly finding time to balance your life activities requires your investment and commitment. The exercises call upon you to think about how you do things now and how you want to do them in the future. Invest the time now. I promise it will be time well spent.

In a book by James Patterson titled Suzanne's Diary for Nicholas there was the most beautiful message that seems to put things into perspective. He wrote,

*"Imagine life is a game in which you are juggling five balls. The balls are called work, family, health, friends, and integrity. And you're keeping all of them in the air. But one day you finally come to understand that work is a rubber ball. If you drop it, it will bounce back. The other four balls – family, health, friends, and integrity – are made of glass. If you drop one of these, it will be irrevocably scuffed, nicked, perhaps even shattered. Once you truly understand the lesson of the five balls, you will have the beginnings of balance in your life."*

May this book help you find the balance you are searching for in your life.

# Introduction

## *This Is My Story*

I awaken during the night with a migraine headache. I've been having more and more of these lately and wonder what could be causing them all of a sudden. I'm always restless and my mind is constantly on work, home or the kids.

"When was the last time I talked to my Mom or other family and friends?" I ask myself. My son has a game he wants me to attend tomorrow, but how can I? I have a big meeting scheduled that will probably take longer than planned so there's no way I'll make it to the game in time. How do I tell him again, I have to miss another important event for him because of work? My head starts to hurt even more now. If only I could get a good night of rest, but that's difficult when I can't shut my mind off. I think I'll take one of the sleeping pills the doctor gave me. That'll help me relax and fall asleep. I'll think about all this tomorrow. Tomorrow I'll figure it all out. But I know that My Tomorrow will have a new set of requests, new tasks to be done, added to what I already can't do today.

"God, help me! Help me want to even wake up to face My Tomorrow." I rhetorically pray. I can't keep going like this. I'm tired. I think my superpowers have run out. What do I do now?

After too many of these types of conversations with myself, I finally said, "ENOUGH! Enough thinking about what I can't do. There's a saying I follow that goes, "If you keep doing things the same way, you'll keep getting the same results." It was time for change. Time to do things differently.

III

To do so meant I had to answer some tough questions such as:

- What's causing me to not handle everything the way I use to?
- What happened to my superpowers?
- How do I get them back?
- What am I willing to change in my life?

I knew I was losing control of my life and the things that were most important to me. I also knew I would never have the peace and happiness I craved until I made some changes. For too long I had allowed work to take precedent over other important matters in my life. Work was my place to escape. If I didn't want to think about the things I wasn't doing at home or with friends and family -didn't want to feel the guilt- then I would work harder. I had a lot of demands on me at work. I also placed a lot of demands on myself.

I had reached a pinnacle point in my career. I was the Vice-President of Human Resources for a major corporation-traveling 30-40% of the time to manage employees in several sites across the US. It was my job to coach and counsel others on ways to be effective in their jobs. Sometimes I even gave advice on how they should find balance in their personal and work life – telling them this would make them even more successful. However, I didn't heed my own advice.

Along with the work demands I also went through several personal life changing events. I went through a divorce and, for the first time, I became a single parent. Quite frankly, this was the scariest job of all. To be responsible for two teenagers, guiding them in their decision making, staying on top of what they were doing or not doing, checking out their friends, having valuable conversations with them and spending a decent quantity of quality time with them. It was more than I was accustomed to and it scared me.

I knew if I didn't handle this job right it could mean the difference between me having two well-rounded, well-adjusted kids who could end up in all sorts of trouble because of my lack of parental support. They couldn't raise themselves and I couldn't raise them during my "mini-breaks" from work. This was non-negotiable for me. I was not going to allow them to suffer from my "workaholic, missing in action most of the time, mind elsewhere habits."

My children are my heart and soul. To lose them, or the opportunity to provide them with every benefit possible, meant losing part of me. It brought me to a crossroad where I had to ask myself, "What did I really want for my life?" A change had to be made. I had to learn how to do things differently. I wanted to do things different.

In addition to all my issues, my brother was very ill and his doctors weren't sure if he would live through year-end. He needed both a kidney and pancreas transplant. I didn't know all this was going on earlier since I hadn't kept in touch with him the way I should have – too busy at work. My health was not the greatest either and I was so young, only forty-two.

During this time, I was building one of my dream homes. I'd never done this alone and all the details of making sure everything went as planned were on my shoulders. And of course, there was my job. As much as I enjoyed my work, I realized I was at a place in life where it wasn't challenging me in a positive way anymore. I wanted something more. I wanted a career, but mostly, "I wanted a life." I believed with all my heart that it was possible to have both and to be successful.

My desire for balance at that time outweighed anything else. I wanted to spend more time doing what really matters the most to me and to those who are important to me.

What was important to me?

- I wanted more time with my family and friends and myself.
- I wanted to spend more time with God, to pray more and help others.
- I wanted to read a novel without falling asleep after the first page.
- I wanted to listen to my children's conversations without my mind drifting to work.
- I wanted to attend their school and sporting functions.
- I wanted to take my Mom out for lunch and spend the entire day with her, giving her my full attention.
- I wanted a good night of rest without medicine.
- I wanted my head and back to stop hurting.

What it boiled down to was, *I wanted a life.* But how was I to get this and still pay the bills. How would I find time to figure this all out? That was the big question.

I finally got to answer that question one day when I had an anxiety attack. I thought I was having a heart attack. Let's just say this was the motivation I needed to find time. My Father died at age 43 from a stroke. I sometimes feared the same could happen to me if I didn't slow down. The problem was I had become a workaholic and I didn't know how to do just that. Just like I didn't know how to rest when my body was in pain.

Somehow I had come to believe that my inability to handle everything meant I was weak and incapable. My ego couldn't handle my not being a superhuman. However, when those pains hit my chest and I couldn't make them go away, another reality set in. If I didn't change how I was doing things it might kill me or handicap me in some way. I drove to my doctor's office and pleaded with her, "Please help me help myself. I can't do this anymore. I'm totally off balance." I felt like the woman on the now infamous commercial who uttered the phrase, "I've fallen and I can't get up."

I took a two-month leave of absence from work to figure it all out. I had to share with my manager what I was going through. This was difficult because my ego was still telling me I was weak for not being able to handle it all. My manager was more than understanding and accommodating to me. It took me almost a month just to decompress and get my mind quiet. Once I did, I began thinking about how I could do things differently at home and at work.

I came up with what I thought was a brilliant plan to cut back my hours, and therefore, be home more for my children and manage all the other activities. My plan was to create a position that allowed me to work part-time, doing what I enjoyed, with less stress. My manager supported my plan and I returned to work. For the first 3 months things were great, but then…

Then my ego stepped in again and said, "You should be able to handle "it all." Take on a few more responsibilities - you don't want others to think you're incapable." Before long I was working full time hours again and making part-time money. I quickly realized I had blow my brilliant plan. The workaholic in me returned. So did the body pains!

Then came scare number two. The chest pains returned. This time I had to have someone take me to the doctor. She immediately took me out of work and told me to make some serious choices. It was another anxiety attack. She warned me, the next time could be the real thing. I took her advice and made one of the toughest decisions ever – I gave up my job.

This is just one of the steps I took to obtain the much needed clarity my life was lacking. There are other things that helped me, which is what this book is all about. My journey to find balance didn't happen in a few short months. It's taken years. I've finally learned what works best for me when it comes to maintaining balance in my life.

Every once in a while I slip back into some old habits but I quickly turn them around by using some of the exercises I'll share in this book. I'm also much more in-tune with my body signals. The body will let you know when you're out of balance. Listen to it.

Have I mastered balancing work, family and personal obligations? Not 100%, but I am much better than I was. There is no more pain, no more anxiety attacks, and no need for medications. No more guilt. Now, I endure great peace, joy, contentment, and finally – *I have a Life.*

# THE
# BALANCING
# ACT

## KEEPING "FIRST-THINGS" FIRST

# Chapter One

# Where Does The Time Go?

J esus
O thers
Y ourself

A very dear friend of mine use to say to me, when I begin to talk about all I have to do, **"KEEP 'FIRST-THINGS' FIRST."** There's something about these words that resonate in my mind and actually cause me to slow down and ask myself, "What am I doing?"

Balancing the many complexities of work and family has become one of the toughest jobs around. It's a juggling act in which you try to do all the things you want and need to do while trying to please everyone and keep your sanity. There is no one magical way to balance it all, nor is it the job of someone else to pull it all together for you. Only **YOU** can do this - to the most practical level of satisfaction YOU need.

Many companies have incorporated work/life initiatives as part of their benefit package. They can provide you resources or perhaps change the scope of your job. But none of this will happen unless you reach out to seek, ask and receive what is being offered.

Before you begin to tackle equalizing the many variables of your life, it is important to first determine *what is taking up your time? Where does the time go?* Complete the following assessment to help you determine your use of time. Your percent need not equal 100. Make your best guess at how much time you think you currently use on the activities.

## EXERCISE #1

### Where Does The Time Go?

| ACTIVITY | CURRENT % ALLOCATION OF TIME | DESIRED GOAL % |
|---|---|---|
| Work | | |
| Children | | |
| Spouse/Significant Other | | |
| Relatives/Aging Parents | | |
| Spiritual | | |
| Personal Leisure "It's All About Me Time" | | |
| Exercise/Health | | |
| Friends | | |
| Vacation/Personal Travel | | |
| Reading/Writing | | |
| TV/Movies | | |
| Housekeeping/Chores | | |
| Community/Clubs | | |
| Education/Training | | |

Need Not Equal 100%

## EXERCISE #1A (Optional Exercise)

In case you find it difficult to estimate the amount of time you spend on the activities in Exercise #1 try this one. Use the Activity Circle on the next page or my Activity Circle Calendar, which can be purchased separately. For the next month, each time you perform one of the activities shown place a check mark (√) in the circle. At the end of the month, do a tally of the check marks made. This will provide you a good estimate of where your time is going. Add activities on the wheel you may be involved in that are not listed.

I post my calendar on the refrigerator each month - its visible and a constant reminder to me to think about where my time is going. At the end of each month I assess what I have done. If I did not focus on any activity as much as I wanted, or did not reach my goals then I change and do things differently the next month.

# The Work/Life Balance Activity Circle

## Month _____

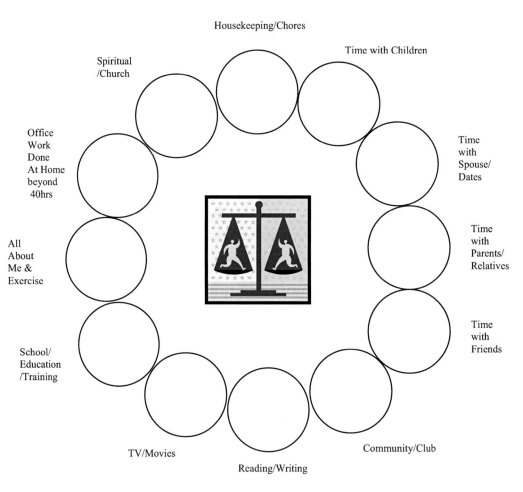

Housekeeping/Chores

Time with Children

Spiritual /Church

Office Work Done At Home beyond 40hrs

Time with Spouse/ Dates

All About Me & Exercise

Time with Parents/ Relatives

School/ Education /Training

Time with Friends

TV/Movies

Community/Club

Reading/Writing

Available for purchase as a Calendar
Includes page for Monthly Goals & Action Plans

## For Singles

If you are single, you may feel many of the activities listed do not apply to you. However, you are feeling the same amount of frustration in finding balance in your life as those who are married and/or have children. If this is the case, replace the activity (s) listed to those that impact you. Many of your activities may deal with more specific personal leisure, sports, exercise or hobbies you want to spend more time on.

## Where Does The Time Go?

| ACTIVITY | CURRENT % ALLOCATION OF TIME | DESIRED GOAL % |
|---|---|---|
| Work | | |
| Significant Other | | |
| Relatives/Aging Parents | | |
| Spiritual | | |
| Personal Leisure "It's All About Me Time" | | |
| Exercise/Health | | |
| Finding a Spouse/Dating | | |
| Friends | | |
| Reading/Writing | | |
| TV/Movies | | |
| Housekeeping/Chores | | |
| Community/Clubs | | |
| Education/Training | | |
| Vacation/Personal Travel | | |

Need Not Equal 100%

## EXERCISE #2

Answer the following questions regarding Exercise #1:

A. Are you satisfied with the current allocation of your time? If yes, why?

B. If not, what people or activities are attributing to this?  As you look at your time allocated for each activity, is there a glaring message that makes you say to yourself, "Wow!  No wonder I'm feeling stressed."

C. Stop for a moment.  Think about what you are currently doing, and what you desire to be doing.   From your assessment create **YOUR** definition of  *"**Balance.**"*  Describe your idea of a well-balanced life.  Keep in mind this definition may change as you grow older or life events change.  You may periodically want to go back and re-define your ideal state of balance.

D.  Once you've completed your definition, go back to Exercise #1 and indicate your ***desired*** percent of time for each activity.

## What Have I Learned So Far

Take a minute to *journal* what you have learned so far from this exercise.  You should have more insight into why you feel *unbalanced* and a better sense of what balance really means to you.

*Chapter Two*

# Priorities!
# How Do You Rate?

Part of balancing your time requires that you establish your priorities and assess how you are doing in maintaining them. Identifying your priorities may be difficult because you may feel that everything is a priority and must be done by you. I have news for you. Everything can't be a priority. YOU can't do everything. You need to determine those things or the *"STUFF"* that is:

**Urgent & Important:** Stuff only you can do and must be done NOW. I refer to these as "My Gotta Do's." They are activities with strict deadlines.

**Important but Less Urgent**: Stuff that must be done but can be accomplished later – no deadlines.

**Nice To Do**: Stuff that is not required and have no deadline. You just feel these activities would be nice to do. These are often those "little things" that eat away our valuable time.

Since your time is so very precious you have to learn how to be selfish about how you spend it.

## EXERCISE #3

Thinking of your current activities at home or work, list those activities or the stuff you consider to be:

A.  Urgent & Important

B.  Important but less Urgent

C.  Nice To Do

D.  How do these line up with your current and desired
    allocation of time from Exercise #1

Have you ever stopped to rate yourself on how effective you manage your job. Usually, we do all kinds of assessments at work that help us determine this. We ask our peers, managers and sometimes employees to rate us on how effective we are. But, what about how effective you are managing things at home with your family. If you asked your family to rate your performance, how effective would they say you are in managing work, family and your personal needs? It's time to find out. This next exercise will work only if your family is totally honest with you and IF you can accept their honest feedback. Brace yourself. This may sting a little!

## EXERCISE # 4

First, rate yourself on how you feel you have done in managing your career/work, managing family needs and taking time to do personal things for yourself.

Next, ask your spouse/ significant other how they would rate you overall in meeting their needs, being there for them, and managing your time with them.

Lastly, if you have children have them rate you on these areas. You can also ask extended family or friends.

Use the rating system of A, B, C, D, or F (school grades).

### How Do I Rate?

| Time Spent On: | Self Rating | Spouse/ Other | Children | Extended Family |
|---|---|---|---|---|
| Career | | | | |
| Family | | | | |
| Personal | | | | |

## For Singles

If you are single you may want to seek input from friends or others who have certain expectations of you.

## How Do I Rate?

## EXERCISE # 4A

| Time Spent On: | Self Rating | Significant Other/ Room-mate | Friends | Family |
|---|---|---|---|---|
| Career | | | | |
| Personal | | | | |
| Other | | | | |

## Exercise #5 - GAP Analysis

The GAP signifies the rating you received by others in comparison to YOUR self-rating.  An acceptable rating differs from one person to the next.  You have to determine what rating is unacceptable to YOU.  That difference is your GAP and may not be aligned with your definition of balance.  For me, any rating that was less than a B was unacceptable.

It's important to find out the reasons behind the ratings you receive.  Ask for feedback and LISTEN.  Don't go into defense mode.  Be open to what they have to say and consider what changes you may need to make to close your GAP.

If you fail to be open to their feedback, the next time you ask – they will tell you what they think you want to hear instead of the truth. Remember, certain things are important to them. This exercise will allow you to see the value they place on your efforts and how well they see you meeting their needs.

**Spouse/Significant Other GAPS**

**Children/Friends GAPS**

**Extended Family GAPS**

You now have more information on what is needed by your family. Consider these as you establish your action plans for creating balance.

# Chapter Three

## It Would Be Nice To Do…But Don't

You probably spend time doing all kinds of "stuff" that is not really *required.* Stuff that you like to do but is not really necessary. Stuff that is not high on your priority list but are simply what I call those *"nice to do"* things. They can easily (and usually do) take up much of your precious and valuable time. Although they may be nice to do, don't do them if they will take away time that could be used on your more important activities. Refer back to activities you listed in Exercise 3C.

It is important to recognize this stuff because we often create our own imbalance and stressors by spending too much time on them. Your imbalance can't be blamed on the family, your manager or anyone else. It's in your mind that this nice to do stuff **must** be done and done ONLY by YOU. And you've convinced yourself they must be done NOW.

There is a solution! **Trade-Offs**. You take the "self-imposed, nice to do stuff" and trade it off for something more important. Creating trade-offs takes courage but the pay-off is more time to use on other important activities.

Some example's of "nice to do" or self-imposed activities and possible trade-off's include:

**Self-Imposed Stuff**
> Constant TV watching

**Trade-off**
> Exercise or play a board game with your family or read a book

**Self-Imposed Stuff**
> Staying late at work to read E-Mails

**Trade-off**
> Go home in time for dinner with the family, read e-mails before bed, after family is asleep

**Other examples of Trade-offs could be:**

| Nice To Do Stuff | Trade-off |
|---|---|
| Cleaning house everyday | Clean once/twice week |
| Having kids in several sports or extracurricular activities | Have them choose one activity |
| Aiming to complete work projects in an extremely aggressive time period you established for appearances | Create a realistic time frame or accept the one given by your boss which allotted you more time to complete |

By letting go of some or all of this stuff you will make room for more important issues in your life.

## EXERCISE #6

Take a moment to identify your self-imposed activities for work and home. List the **"nice to do"** stuff you have been doing. Then attempt to identify some tradeoffs you can make and what gains will be obtained as a result. Consider the activities listed in Exercise 1 and 3C as you make your list.

| Stuff I Will Trade-Off | To Gain |
|---|---|
| **Example-** Buying new clothes this month | Money for a housekeeper |
| **Example -** ½ hour of sleep | 30 minutes to exercise |
| | |
| | |
| | |
| | |
| | |
| | |
| | |
| | |
| | |

# EXERCISE #6

Take a moment to identify your self-imposed activities for work and home. List the **"nice to do"** stuff you have been doing. Then attempt to identify some tradeoffs you can make and what gains will be obtained as a result. Consider the activities listed in Exercise 1 and 3C as you make your list.

| Stuff I Will Trade-Off | To Gain |
|---|---|
| **Example-** Buying new clothes this month | Money for a housekeeper |
| **Example -** ½ hour of sleep | 30 minutes to exercise |
| | |
| | |
| | |
| | |
| | |
| | |
| | |
| | |
| | |

## Chapter Four

## "First-Things" First

Just what do I mean by "First-Things" First? I am referring to keeping those things that matter the most to you in life ahead of everything else.

For me, that meant my relationship with God, my children, my family and my friends. These relationships have always been important to me. However, somewhere along the way, I allowed my career to take precedent over them. Afterwards, I noticed things started to go wrong. I rarely had enough time for my family. Friends and family would call me, I always told them, "I'll get back to you." but I rarely did. Time for myself was virtually non-existent. Even when I was at home my mind, as I'm sure yours has been, was on the job. I finally had to stop and ask myself, "What are you doing?" I wasn't happy with this life style, yet; I found it hard to put an end to it. I came to a realization:

I was addicted to my job.
I was a workaholic.

I had to step back and ask myself some important questions. Propose them to yourself.

**EXERCISE #7**

Answer the following:

    A.  What are your "First-Things?"

    B.  Are you spending enough time on your "First-Things?" Is this reflected in Exercises 1 and 3?

C. How often do you find yourself either contemplating about or involving yourself in activities that aren't your "First-Things?"   Why or Why Not?  Refer back to Exercise 5 – GAP Analysis.  Could this be attributing to your gaps?

D. Who (not what) determines the amount of time you commit to your "First-Things?"

As you go forward, ask yourself when you get busy in activities,

Am I doing what matters most?
Am I keeping 'First-Things' First?"

If the answer is, "No" then regroup and start all over again. Quickly forgive yourself, never give up and move forward.

You've identified what's most important to you – Your "First Things." This should create the motivation needed to attack that "other stuff " that keeps getting in the way and keeps you from finding balance.

Another factor to keep in mind - what you strongly *believe* in as well as *say* is what you will usually get. Your thoughts and words must support your desire. From this point forward make this promise to yourself – I will only think and say positive, re-affirming words regarding my efforts in devoting the desired amount of time to my "First-Things."

Now, visualize yourself having the time, energy, money and support to do what YOU want to do. Believe you can. Start saying each day, *"I am balancing my work, family and personal time more and more each day. I will make my "First Things" my first priority."*

## Chapter Five

# Learn To Say "NO" And Not Feel Guilty

Saying No! Much easier said than done. Why is this so hard to do? We would rather inconvenience ourselves than to tell someone, "Sorry, I can't help you."

If you don't learn to use this very important two-letter word when necessary, others will infringe upon your precious time. Friends, family, and co-workers will help themselves to your time. Yet, they may not be there to help make that time up for you. Your time is precious and limited. Don't give it away. How do you say, No?

First, begin to examine every request you get to do something, then ask yourself the following questions:

- Is this something I'm required to do?
- Will this put me behind in my work and add undue pressure in meeting my deadlines? If so, – just say, "No."
- Will this take me away from something I was planning to do with my family? If so, say, "No."

- What do I gain personally or professionally if I take on this task? If the answer is, "Little to nothing" then say, No."

- Will saying, "No" produce a negative outcome, one I can't afford to have? If the answer is Yes, it will or it might "possibly" produce a negative outcome, then determine what you can adjust, give up doing or trade-off that will allow you to do the task and not leave you feeling guilty or stressed. If the answer is, "No," then say so.

Second, learn to barter. If someone asks you for help, determine if there is something they can do for you in return. This may not be necessary all the time, however, it can be a good way to find help when you need it. You may be surprised at how willing the person will be to return the favor.

You may come across people who will take advantage of your inability to say No. They will ask for your help, knowing you won't say No. To stop this routine – next time they make a request, ask them to do something for you at the same time. This will condition them to help you in return or stop them from taking advantage of you.

## EXERCISE #8:

Over the next month, practice saying, "No" when appropriate and expedient. Examine every request. Learn to barter and look for opportunities to gain help when necessary. Protect your time as if your life depended on it. If you want to have a balanced life your ability to say "NO" will help get you there. Also, refer back to previous Exercises to determine if there are activities you should be saying "No" to more often.

Journal the outcome of saying, "No." What did you gain? How was it received?

## What Have I Learned So Far

Take a minute to *journal* what you have learned so far from this exercise. You should have more insight into why you feel unbalanced and a better sense of what balance really means to you.

# Chapter Six

## Is Your Career In The Way?

For most, having a career is necessary in order to survive. We need resources. Our jobs are usually the means by which we obtain them. However, you must assess if your career is getting in the way of your finding balance.

It can be very easy to allow our careers to become more than a means to achieve survival. It's true that the more we obtain the more comfortable our survival is. What we need to determine is how much we are willing to sacrifice to obtain greater comfort and more balance.

Earlier you assessed the amount of time you expend on your career. Let's explore that a little further. Consider the following aspects of your career. Are you in a position that:

- Requires you to travel a lot?
- That's very demanding?
- That requires you to work long hours?
- Is an obstacle to applying adequate time to your "First-Things?"

If you determine that your career is pushing **against** your family or personal time then its time to re-evaluate your current career situation.

## EXERCISE #9

Answer the following questions that may apply to your situation:

A. What will you gain, lose or compromise if you **continue** in your current position?

| Gain | Lose or Compromise |
| --- | --- |
|  |  |

B. What will you gain, lose or compromise if you **leave** your current position?

| Gain | Lose or Compromise |
| --- | --- |
|  |  |

C. Can my family and I afford the consequences that may arise from a career/position change (in the event of a pay decrease)?  Will I/we be able to manage things financially?

D. Am I striving to achieve a career/position that will require more time than what I currently invest in my job?

E. How much time and effort will be involved in searching for a new position? Consider time to search for positions, interview scheduling, communicating with current management, etc. How will this impact your current use of time?

F. Will my company be agreeable to the idea of me adjusting my position or hours? Will they consider creating a new position that will give me what I want?

G. Should I remain in my current position? If "Yes," why? If "No," why not?

Many people answer question number 9F without even testing the waters by approaching their manager to allow them to do their job differently. You may be pleasantly surprised how willing employers are becoming in their efforts to help their employees balance work and family. They recognize the benefits of working with you on this. Don't be afraid to look into this and make a request.

## What Worked For Me

Before I made the decision to leave my position as I described earlier, I made a request to take on a job I had designed. It was a position that would allow me to do the things I most enjoyed in my profession. I knew if I worked within an area I most enjoyed it would relieve some pressure and stress while keeping me challenged. I created a job description and presented it to my manager. I boldly asked him to give it careful consideration since the outcome would be a "Win-Win" situation for everyone involved.

At the time of my request there were other people occupying the positions and doing the work I wanted to do. This should have made me talk myself out of making the request. However, I believed my plan would help me keep "First-Things" first. Therefore, I persevered.

What happen next was nothing short of miraculous. Within a few weeks of my request, two individuals, that were doing the work I wanted to do, left their positions. One moved on to another position and the other left the company for personal reasons. Keep in mind; at the time of my request, I had no idea that these two people would be leaving.

Needless to say, that work still had to be done. Guess who got to do it? Yes, I got what I wanted. So what's the moral of this story?

Don't stop yourself from doing something just because of how it looks currently. You never know what might happen to cause events to line up in your favor when you are attempting to keep "First-Things" first.

After completing Exercise # 9 you should have a clearer outlook of your current career/job and how it impacts your personal life.  If you've determined that a career or a position change is necessary it's time to create your plan of action.

## EXERCISE #10:

Using the Career Action Plan chart on the following page, list the changes you will need to make in your current work situation; what specific actions you must take and when you will begin to do so.

Writing things down helps foster accountability.  It can also serve as a reminder to you of what you promised to do for yourself.  By making these changes you are getting closer to finding the balance you are looking for at work and home.

# Career Action Plan

| Changes To Make | What I Need To Do | When "Date" |
|---|---|---|
| **Example:** Shorter Hours | Approach my manager with a proposal | Immediately |
| | | |
| | | |
| | | |
| | | |
| | | |
| | | |

# Chapter Seven

# When All Else Fails

Hopefully you will never get to the point of having to make a decision to leave a job you love, deprive your family of your time and attention, give up the idea of having a personal life or return to school for that degree you've always wanted. There are other options before doing any of the above. It's a personal decision that only you can make.

Sadly, I have actually seen people make the decision to leave their family in order to keep their career. Others do nothing but go to work and rarely go out to enjoy life or have relationships. Some did not physically leave their family, rather, they just mentally disconnect. They made themselves believe it didn't matter. They left everything up to their spouse, family, or the babysitter. Who really suffers in this situation? Everyone.

If this sounds like you, don't be surprised if one day, when you look for your family or partner you find them MIA: Missing In Action. They may conclude that since you aren't there for them, they will no longer be there for you.

The price of failing to balance things can cause various issues.  Losing your family is the worst of them.

Listed below are a few personal and professional risks:

- Become a hopeless workaholic
- Loss of Job
- Loss of focus and attention
- Mental/physical exhaustion (burn-out)
- Health Issues
- Divorce
- Loss of respect from those that matter the most
- Stress, irritation, worry, anxiety
- Loss of intimacy and sexual desires
- Missed special family activities

Unfortunately, this list can easily be extended.  However, you can avoid these risks from occurring if you can:

- Be creative
- Be willing to try something different
- Get help
- Acknowledge when you have failed at something
- Forgive yourself
- And start over again

I always tell others as well as myself, "If you keep doing things the same way, you'll keep getting the same results."  If your results so far have not been helpful or positive, then it's time to do something different.  Before making any decisions, make sure you have identified all your "Trade-offs."

The following chapters address options for creating positive changes in your life - both at work and at home.

# *Chapter Eight*

# Balance Options At Work

**Experiment with other ways to get your job done.**

In this chapter you will need to get your creative juices flowing to come up with an action plan promoting activities conducive to finding a peaceful, yet, productive balance while on the job.

There's always more than one way to get a job done. Because you've been doing something the same way for a period of time doesn't mean it can't change. That old saying "this is the way we've always done it" should be removed from your vocabulary.

We've established that you may need to reconsider the current career path you are traveling. Here are a few things to consider while on your journey. Think of them as Roadside Assistance!

## EXERCISE #11

A. List below some alternatives to getting your work done. Think "Out of the Box" for methods that will create more time for your "First-Things."

*Example, can you bring in a college intern to perform certain tasks (requires little to no pay and in return you coach them and help them learn new skills – great trade-off)?*

B. Ask your manager or co-workers for suggestions. Find out what works well for them and list their responses below.

## What Worked For Me

My work allows me the ability to work from home. I love it because I am not limited to a 9-5 schedule. I plan my tasks based on my high peak times when I am more alert, creative and productive.

My peak times are between 8AM and 2PM. So I use this time to call my customers or write programs. Between 2PM and 5PM my brain has "checked out" and it takes me longer to get things done. During this time I take care of some of my household chores or read e-mails. My second peak time is around 7pm and I can work until 1 or 2AM. I use this time to do research, paperwork, reading and computer work.

I also completed Exercise 3 to help me prioritize what I was doing. I made a list of those activities that were urgent and important, and important but less urgent. I realized that many of the things I was doing was "Nice To Do" stuff. It was stuff I thought was important but the family didn't appreciate or need. I immediately stopped doing these tasks. I felt some relief and gained some time.

The toughest thing for me was learning to say "No." Interestingly it was not so much saying "No" to others but telling myself "NO." I was my worst enemy. My perfectionist attitude caused me to spend too much time doing less important stuff. I thought if I got the small stuff out of the way first, then I'd have time to focus on the big stuff. Instead, the small stuff used up too much of my time. I had to stop. Letting go of that small stuff and learning to say, "No" saved my day.

**Trust Others to Help You and Delegate**.

Why do we think we have to do it all?  Why is it so hard to ask others for help? These are important questions to consider.

We often fail to do so because we don't trust that others will do the task as well as we can.  It may be we like being in control or we feel it will take too long to train someone else.

Whatever the reason, you must face the reality that *you can't do it all!*   There are others who may be able to help you carry out your responsibilities.  All you have to do is ask.

If you're in a position to delegate tasks, doing so gives you more free time.  Go ahead, give yourself permission to assign work to others and stop thinking you have to do it all. Why try to figure everything out yourself if you don't have to?


**EXERCISE #12**

Using the Work Task chart on the next page -- list as many work tasks you perform now.  Then ask yourself the following questions about each task:
- Does this task add value to my customers, company or career?
- How much time do I spend doing this task?
- Can someone else either help with or do this job? If so, to whom can you delegate it?

# Work Tasks

| Activity | Amount of Time It Takes To Do | Does it add Value to anyone Y or N | Must Do Myself Y or N | Delegate or Share Y or N & WHO |
|---|---|---|---|---|
| | | | | |
| | | | | |
| | | | | |
| | | | | |
| | | | | |
| | | | | |
| | | | | |
| | | | | |
| | | | | |

Once you list all the tasks then apply the following simple formula:

For those things that do not add value, **STOP DOING THEM**

For those things you can delegate, **START DELEGATING**

For those things you can share, **START SHARING**

The point is to stop doing unnecessary tasks even if its something you've been doing since the beginning. If that activity does not add value to your customers or company you are wasting your time, energy and money (both your company's and possibly yours) by performing that task.

To delegate shows you trust someone. It allows others to grow and learn new skills as well as adds to the level of job satisfaction. Happy employees = a happy company. Most importantly delegating frees time up for you to do other important things. The same holds true for those tasks you can share with someone else.

Hopefully, you've identified some activities you can delegate, share or stop doing. If so, your stress level should be lower. You should feel the difference. Now all you need to do is put your plan into action.

Identify to whom you will delegate those tasks. Meet with them to make the transition. DO NOT PROCRASTINATE. The sooner you follow through the sooner you will have additional time for what's more important. You will be closer to creating the balance you need.

## Move into another position.

This could be a lateral position or a concentrated effort to obtain a promotion. Search for one that is obviously less stressful and time consuming. Either should allow you to find time for personal activities while still contributing to the organization.

Let's face it, there are some jobs in an organization where the position pays the same, however, the workload is different. You may see some of your peers leave at the end of the day at a reasonable hour but you can't because the demands of your position are greater. Why not move into one of those positions until your life is more balanced?

## Take a lower level position.

No one wants to consider this when they are trying to build a career and climb up the corporate ladder. After all, who wants to climb down? However, this may be a solution for your situation. Should you have to go this route remember you're not committing to it forever. It's just for this season in your life.

Once your family and other life issues are settled you can always start the climb back up the ladder. Many people have done this. They have consciously removed themselves from the high visibility position to start a family, help a sick parent or a variety of other reasons. Later, they went back after their affairs were in order. They made valuable contributions in the lower level position and their career did not suffer.

The best time to make a move like this is when you are at the top because that is how people will remember you. Be sure to involve your manager and/ or Human Resource manager in your decision making process.

Let them know the reason behind your decision as well as your desire to return to your position later. If your company *values you*, they will understand, respect your decision, and be there to support you when you are ready to come back to the level you left.

Though this may be a necessary step for you to make, it is imperative that you keep in mind – **this is a serious step**. It is not something that should be done hastily or in a fit of anger or disappointment resulting from some negative aspect of your position. While there are no guarantees of this being a successful direction in which to go, it may be one that you need to consider. Just be sure to do so wisely.

## When all else fails, find another company to work for . . . or start your own!

You might find another company that will allow you to do the kind of work you enjoy within the boundaries you have set for balance. You won't know until you try it. Sometimes you have to step out of your comfort zone. "Get out of the boat and walk on the water" as I sometimes think of it. When your motives for making a change like this are right, such as making time for family, yourself and other important events, things line up in your favor. What you thought was impossible becomes possible.

True control comes when you run the show. Starting your own company will allow you to make the rules and set your hours. This is the truly ***ultimate*** position. However, this is not realistic for everyone. It takes great discipline and - to put it simply - guts to venture out on your own. It can bring on a whole new set of stressors. But I must say the payoffs are fabulous when it all comes together.

## *What Worked For Me*

*I came to the place in my career that in order to keep "First-things" First, I had to make the decision to leave the company. I was in a "when all else fails" situation. I tried working part time and still found myself unable to find balance. I knew it was time for a radical change.*

*When I saw the things most important to me slipping away because of my work, I had to give up the work I loved because it was killing me in more ways than one. I had to leave. I got up the nerve to talk to my manager about what was going on and he understood.*

*My imbalance was due to multiple issues, which caused me to deal with all of the high stress issues that can hit a person's life. I was a single parent for the first time and quite honestly the thought of raising two teenagers scared me more than any work assignment I ever had. I was going through a divorce, which could have caused me to lose custody of my children to their father. I was building a new home. I had just started a new position as Vice President of Human Resources in my company, and relocated from Colorado to Virginia. My only brother had been informed that he would not live through the end of the year unless he received a kidney and pancreas transplant. Moreover, I was dealing with some physical illnesses myself.*

*To say I had too much on me at that time in my life is an understatement. No one at work had any idea I was dealing with all these issues. I managed to keep it to myself and it had not affected my job performance.*

*Eventually it started taking me longer to get things done. I began to dislike the work I loved. I couldn't focus for long periods of time and then fear came. I feared failing at everything. Feared losing my kids' love and attention and what I believed was my last chance at being a mom. This was simply too much to bear.*

*When I did Exercise 5 – How Do I Rate, in Chapter 2 - I failed. I considered any rating by my children or myself, that was less than A or B to be failing. I could see my kids slipping away. They were putting up walls against me to protect themselves. It was easier for my children to do that than to believe their Mom loved her work more than them.*

*I felt this was my last chance with them. I wanted an "A" so I made one of my toughest decisions ever. I left my company.*

*I left at what was the pinnacle of my career. I was at the top and the opportunity was present to go even higher. I knew, however, to pursue anything more at that time in my life would be disastrous. I knew if I left then, I would be remembered favorably and would have a good chance of being re-hired one day if that is what I wanted. I also knew that if I stayed, given my situation at the time - the stress I was under and the same responsibilities - my performance was going to suffer and I might be asked to leave.*

*Sometimes the best answer is right in front of your eyes. You just have to look at it. Take a deep breath and "just do it."*

# Chapter Nine

# Balance Options At Home

## Involve Your Family in Creating Balance

Do you think you are the only one who can figure out how to get everything done?  If your answer is "Yes," let me be the one to tell you that you are fooling yourself.  Finding balance at home will involve allowing others to help you.  There are many options to consider that do not have to include you.

Just as you had to ask for help in managing your work activities, the same must be done at home.  Instead of your employees or co-workers helping you, utilize your family, friends or outside help whenever you are feeling overwhelmed and off balance.  You'll be surprised at the ideas that others can come up with in order to help you.

We often think we know what our family needs, but when was the last time you asked them what they needed?  I remember thinking I had to cook a meal every night or the family would feel I am not being a good mother and wife.

Each night I ran home from work, threw my briefcase down, threw a pan on the stove, changed my clothes while the pan was getting hot, threw a load of laundry in the washer and picked up stuff lying around - All the while pouting and complaining about how no one was helping me.

When I finally said something about this to my family they replied, "Who asked you to come home and cook each night? We usually aren't even hungry and don't want to eat a full course meal each night." Here I was thinking they wanted this when it did not even matter to them if I did it or not. It never occurred to me to find out why they only ate half or none of the food I cooked.

Ask your family what they want or need from you. What are their expectations of you? Don't be surprised if they're different from *your* thoughts of their expectations. Make adjustments based on what they tell you. If they want or need more than you can deliver then delegate tasks to other members of the family or look for trade-offs.

The following exercise will allow you, your family or partner to gain a better understanding of what each person is doing to support each other and establish realistic expectations. You will also begin to identify things you can hand-off to someone outside of the family such as a relative, a handyperson or housekeeper.

## EXERCISE #13

Using the chart on the next page, list the household tasks and expectations each member of the family has of each other.  Discuss each person's expectations calmly.   Find out why the task is important to them and who should be responsible.  Then discuss alternatives if the task is an unrealistic expectation.

If the tasks are unrealistic or cannot be done by the person suggested then identify who should be responsible for that task going forward.  This will allow everyone to see all that has to be done to keep a family going and to meet everyone's needs.

Example:  Lets say there is an expectation from each member of the family that Mom is responsible for doing the laundry.  Mom, however, feels this task should be rotated each week and everyone should share this responsibility.
You would list it on the chart as follows:

## Home/Family Tasks

| Expectations/Tasks | Who Is/Should Do This | | | |
| --- | --- | --- | --- | --- |
| | Self | Spouse/ Partner/ Roommate | Kids/ Friend/ Family Mbr | New Responsible Person(s) OR External Source |
| Example: Do the laundry | X | | | All - rotate weekly |
| | | | | |
| | | | | |
| | | | | |
| | | | | |
| | | | | |
| | | | | |

# Home/Family Tasks

| Expectations/Tasks | Who Is/Should Do This | | |
| --- | --- | --- | --- |
| | Self | Spouse/ Partner/ Roomate | Kids/ Friend/ Family Mbr | New Responsible Person(s) OR External Resource |
| | | | | |
| | | | | |
| | | | | |
| | | | | |
| | | | | |
| | | | | |
| | | | | |
| | | | | |

## Don't Hold Back in Letting Others Know You Need Help

When responsibilities begin to pile up on you it's time to let someone know you need help. Asking for help can be difficult for some people. Is it difficult for you? If so, ask yourself "Why?" Aim to discover why you feel you are the only one who can handle things - then address those feelings carefully to see if they are justified or just in your mind.

Often family and friends can tell when you are over your head and want to help you. They may not offer to help if you give the impression you don't need or want any help. They may be wary of offering because of their uncertainty of your reaction or they are just waiting for you to ask them.

If asking for help is difficult for you, the best solution is to start practicing. Take small steps. Begin by asking your neighbor to take your child to soccer practice since they are taking their child or offer to rotate the chore.

Ask friends - who may be trying to balance their lives as well - if they want to work together with you and use trade-offs to get free time. For example: you may take their kid one weekend a month, as a trade-off, the next time, they take yours. This will give both of you some free time you normally would not have.

## Quality vs. Quantity of Time with Family

I've heard people say, "It's not the amount of time you spend with your family as much as the quality of time that matters." There is some truth to this although when it comes to children, they want and demand both. The key is to make the best use of the time you have with them.

You should guard this time like it was gold. Don't allow anything to infringe upon it. Some things you can do to make family time more rewarding:

- Shut off your cell phone, pager, any electronic item.

- Tell friends or family when you have plans with your family and they should be considerate of them.

- Don't multi-task during this time. Too many distractions will take you away from them.

- Shut your mind down from work and other issues or thoughts and focus on them.

- Spend time doing what **they** want to do, if unsure, don't assume - ask them.

- Play games instead of watch TV or watch their favorite show with them.

- Act interested in what they are saying and doing – even if you aren't.

- Do something your spouse or significant other enjoys without complaints.

- Let them know when you are giving up doing something else to spend quality time with them (without adding any conditions of guilt). It allows them to see how much they mean to you.

- Tell them and show them how important they are to you. Back this up with plenty of hugs & kisses - no matter how old they are!

## Resources To Help Lighten The Load

Since you may not be able to do it all yourself it may be to your benefit to start looking for resources outside the home to help you with certain things.

I have a simple philosophy when it comes to certain types of work; if I can pay someone to do something I don't like to do then I will. I will not do lawn or repair work. I will make whatever trade-off is necessary to save enough money in order to pay someone else to do these things.

Get creative and think of ways you can hand-off work to free up time for yourself. The point is to stop thinking you have to do it all. There are others who can do things as well as, if not better than you. Find them. Hire them (if you can afford to do so). Barter with them. Do whatever you can to make it a win-win situation.

### Other Options To Consider:
- Hire a college student to help the kids with homework.

- Hire kids in the neighborhood to take care of the lawn.

- Bring in a transfer student from overseas to live with you while they attend school.

- Help your children learn a second language.
  Hire an in-home caregiver from another country and have the person speak his/her language around your kids to teach them.

- Put an ad in your church bulletin or local Newspaper for a Caregiver or Adopted Grandmother to care for your "loving family and home."

## What Worked For Me

To help lighten my load, I hired a wonderful Caregiver to come into my home to take care of my children. I found that the money I paid the daycare was enough to pay someone to come to my home and care for them until I came home. I looked for a Nanny that was a "grandmother" type. I found her at a church through a friend. She arrived before I left in the morning, which meant I did not have to wake the kids up, wash, dress or feed them. I saved at least an hour of time doing this and I used this time to sleep in late or go in to work earlier so I could leave early.

My Caregiver made sure the kids had dinner, helped them with homework so that when I came home in the evening all I had to do was to play and talk with them, spend time with my husband (at the time) or use the time for myself. This took tremendous stress off of me. She also helped with light housework and laundry. I made a trade-off with her. She did not have a washing machine at her home and had to go to the laundry-mat to wash her clothes. I allowed her to use my machine in exchange for her doing some of the housework.

I'll never forget the day my Caregiver asked if I would mind if she cooked more often for the family and not just the kids. I looked at her with the biggest smile and said, "You can have the kitchen!" I told her to redecorate it in anyway that best suited her and I would give her money to buy the groceries. She could buy and cook whatever she wanted. Cooking is just something I did not find any pleasure in doing and would gladly trade-off. She loved to cook and this gave her something to do during the day when the kids where at school. We never ate as well before this and there was rarely food left on the plate, as it had been when I cooked. She also was able to stay overnight if I was called out of town, which greatly reduced my stress level of being away on business.

Take a minute to *journal* what you have learned so far from this exercise. You should have more insight into why you feel balanced but also a better sense of what balance really means to you.

# Chapter Ten

# Finding Time For Yourself

One of the biggest mistakes we make is while trying to take care of everyone else's needs we fail to take care of our own personal needs. You must build in time to just get away by yourself and do something special just for YOU.

When is the last time you did this? What did you do? How often do you take time for yourself?

If you do this often and have built into your schedule what I call your **"ALL ABOUT ME"** time then A+ for you! Finding time for you is critical. It will help you relieve stress while staying friendly towards others.

If you find it impossible to do this because of work or family demands then you need to give it a higher priority. We often fail to do for ourselves because it makes us feel selfish. We have been taught to put others needs before our own. Although this is good to do at times – it's also good to put self first.

If you feel guilty about spending time doing something for yourself when you could be doing something for someone else – STOP. You deserve to reward yourself for all your hard work. You deserve time to rejuvenate and re-energize yourself. You deserve time to be alone, to rest, be at peace, to be pampered.

Instead of thinking about what you wish you could do for you, start doing things just for you. It can be as simply as a daily evening walk alone or as big as a trip away alone or with friends.

## EXERCISE #14

Answer the following:

On the next page list your "All About Me" activities you will do for yourself and how often you will do them - daily, weekly, yearly, etc. Again, get creative with things you can do. Make a commitment to do these things for YOU. Let the family know when you will be taking this time and get them to buy-in and support you when your special time approaches. Indicate what you can realistically do now, along with your goals of what you'd like to do in the future.

## "All About Me" Activities

| Things To Do For Myself | Frequency: Daily, Weekly, Monthly, Yearly | Desired Goals for the Future |
|---|---|---|
| Example: Get a massage, manicure, pedicure | 2 times/year | Monthly |
| | | |
| | | |
| | | |
| | | |
| | | |
| | | |
| | | |
| | | |
| | | |
| | | |
| | | |

## *What Worked For Me*

I use to feel so guilty whenever I took time to do things just for me. I would go shopping for myself, head home, happily, with all my new items. Along the way, guilt would come when I realized - I had not brought my husband or kids anything. I would either, return to the store and make a purchase for them, or hide my items in the trunk of the car and act like I brought nothing. Silly, right? Why I felt guilty and selfish, I do not know considering, I was always buying for them.

I had to convince myself that I deserved to treat myself good. If I didn't, it may never happen. I brought a self-help book that gave me great ideas of things to do - *just for me*. I didn't just read the book. I took the Authors advice and tried out several of the suggestions. I told myself it was okay to be selfish, to take care of me, and to pamper me. I worked hard for my money – why shouldn't I spend it on me too.

I would take nice long baths, with candles, music and would lock the door. In the beginning the family inevitably would call me for something, knock on the door every few minutes, asking, "how much longer will you be." Finally, I let them know – "if you want me to be nice to you, it would be wise for you to stop interrupting my "All About Me" time. They got the message and backed off.

Eventually, the guilt left. Now, I selfishly give myself all the time, pampering, love and gifts I can. I deserve it. I won't deny myself. I've identified a number of ways to spend time with myself such as: walks in the park, read a book at the lake, I even take my work to the park – laptop and all, find a picnic table and enjoy the sun, lake and fresh air.

Your "ALL ABOUT ME" time is precious and you should be very selfish when it comes to these activities. Try not to be so quick to give this time up to others – which is easy to do. You've put yourself last most of the time, only to find out – you have no more time. Make time for yourself. You'll feel better and so will your family.

# In Conclusion

I've shared with you my ideas, concepts, practices and techniques that have been useful in my life. If you feel your situation is more extreme and more help is necessary it may be time to find a personal work/life coach to help you on a one-on-one basis. Whatever your situation, I commend you for recognizing the need for a change and urge you to stay vigilant in your quest to master "The Balancing Act." Remember to **KEEP "FIRST-THINGS" FIRST.**

One last exercise to help you put everything you've learned all together. If you truly want to be successful in finding balance you MUST establish some goals. You've done this in Exercises 1, 2, 10 and 14.

You've also received input from family and friends regarding their expectations and needs from Exercises 4, 5 and 13.

You've identified several trade-offs and identified times when you need to start saying "NO" from Exercises 6, and 8.

You've given careful consideration to what you gain or lose in maintaining, changing, or giving up your current position to obtain balance. This was determined, in Exercises 9, 10, 11 and 12.

Most importantly, being good to YOU. You have to feel good about YOU to make change happen. You have to be rested, energetic and positive. You have to have the right attitude and believe you can find the balance you have been searching for and as you defined in Exercise 1 and 2.

Lastly, the most important and final step is establishing specific goals and action plans you will follow once you put this book down.

It's time to create your **"Work/Life Balance Action Plan." Your Final Exercise #15 - on next page.**

You must establish realistic goals and action steps for yourself. Involve others to assist you if needed. Don't be afraid to ask for help. Be diligent and determined to succeed in finding balance. Never give up!

It may be helpful to have someone, a friend or family member, who will hold you accountable. I call them my Accountability Agent. Once you have completed your Action Plan give them a copy. Their job is to check in with you periodically to see how you are doing, motivate and encourage you to follow through on your plan. Hiring a Career/Life Coach can assist you as well.

**My Accountability Agent will be:**

_____

**Good Luck, God Bless and Don't Give Up.
You can do what you believe you can do.**

*You Can Balance Work and Family.*

# Exercise 15

## Work Life Balance Action Plan

| Goals<br>Changes To Make | Action Steps<br>What I Need To Do | When<br>"Date" |
|---|---|---|
| | | |
| | | |
| | | |
| | | |
| | | |
| | | |
| | | |

# Exercise 15

## Work Life Balance Action Plan

| Goals<br>Changes To Make | Action Steps<br>What I Need To Do | When<br>"Date" |
|---|---|---|
|  |  |  |
|  |  |  |
|  |  |  |
|  |  |  |
|  |  |  |
|  |  |  |
|  |  |  |

# Exercise 15

## Work Life Balance Action Plan

| Goals<br>Changes To Make | Action Steps<br>What I Need To Do | When<br>"Date" |
|---|---|---|
| | | |
| | | |
| | | |
| | | |
| | | |
| | | |
| | | |

# Notes & Reflections
## How This Book Has Helped Me

# APPENDIX
# Chapter Exercises

# Comments, Suggestions
# You Can Offer Others

We'd love to hear your ideas, suggestions and experiences
that have worked for you. It's how we learn best – from each
other. *PLEASE* share what's worked for you and send to us.
Thank you in advance for helping others find work/life balance.

_____

_____

_____

_____

_____

_____

_____

_____

_____

_____

_____

_____

_____

_____

_____

_____

_____

_____

_____

Send to us at www.jhbvisions.com or fax to 804-639-9884

# About the Author

J. Harrison Blackwell prides herself on her strong ability to motivate and inspire people to make positive changes in their lives. She is a recognized authority in the area of personal and career growth and development.

As the President & CEO of Visions + Solutions, she has traveled the nation as a motivational speaker, corporate trainer, career/life & business coach and well known author. Her clients include International Fortune 500 companies such as General Electric, Genworth Financial, AT&T, and CSX Transportation. She also works with several Universities, State, Federal and Not-for-Profit organizations.

Her latest book, The Balancing Act: Keeping "First-Things" First, depicts her personal and professional experiences in addition to providing strategies to creating and maintaining a balanced life.

She is a native of Norfolk, Virginia and earned a BS degree in Business Administration from Norfolk State University in Norfolk, Virginia. She currently resides in Richmond, Virginia.

> To contact J. Harrison Blackwell or to request information on speaking, facilitating, coaching, and consulting services, call (804) 639-9886 or e-mail jbvisions@aol.com. Please visit her web site at www.jhbvisions.com.

# Other Books
# Written By The Author


## *"His Voice"*
## *My Fall Retreat With Father*

A Memoir of the conversations with My Father – GOD. While on a fall retreat he relayed messages to me that have left a lasting impressions upon my heart as he explained so many of my life experiences, trials and my walk with him.


## *"Visioning For Success"*
## *A Career & Leadership*
## *Development Program*

A guide and handbook to help you find success in your career and life. Used as a training module in businesses and universities, consisting of several stand-alone topics or can be delivered as one program to enhance and develop critical leadership skills and assist you in managing your career. May be purchased as a Train-the-Trainer workbook, as a self-paced learning tool and as a motivational or seminar topic.

Visit our website to purchase books or tapes or contact us at:

http://www.jhbvisions.com

E-Mail: jbvisions@aol.com

Call at 804-639-9886

# NOTES

# NOTES

# NOTES

# NOTES